THE
and

What are the eerie ... round the Royal P... What is the mysterious shape with a huge head and staring eyes that lurks in the attic? Could it be the Ghost of Incrediblania?

This dramatic question introduces more unexpected adventures in the mythical and amusing Kingdom of Incrediblania. Readers of *The Dribblesome Teapots* and *The Home-Made Dragon* will not be surprised to find the King and Queen of that troublesome country dealing with the Frantic Phantom with their usual commonsense and good humour, as well as getting plenty of fun out of such homely matters as the royal washing (or should Incrediblania have a launderette?) and even from such grave matters as an attempted takeover by that arch villain Count Bakwerdz.

Lots of old friends (and enemies) and lots of laughs for mythical monarch fanciers from eight or so up.

The Frantic Phantom
and Other Incredible Stories

Norman Hunter

Illustrations by
Geraldine Spence

PUFFIN BOOKS
in association with The Bodley Head

Puffin Books, Penguin Books Ltd, Harmondsworth, Middlesex, England
Penguin Books, 625 Madison Avenue, New York, New York 10022, U.S.A.
Penguin Books Australia Ltd, Ringwood, Victoria, Australia
Penguin Books Canada Ltd, 41 Steelcase Road West, Markham, Ontario, Canada
Penguin Books (N.Z.) Ltd, 182–190 Wairau Road, Auckland 10, New Zealand

—

First published by The Bodley Head 1973
Published in Puffin Books 1976
Reprinted 1976 (twice)

—

Copyright © Norman Hunter, 1973
Illustrations © The Bodley Head Ltd, 1973

—

Made and printed in Great Britain by
Cox & Wyman Ltd, London, Reading and Fakenham
Set in Intertype Baskerville

This book is sold subject to the condition
that it shall not, by way of trade or otherwise,
be lent, re-sold, hired out, or otherwise circulated
without the publisher's prior consent in any form of
binding or cover other than that in which it is
published and without a similar condition
including this condition being imposed
on the subsequent purchaser

Contents

1.	The Frantic Phantom	7
2.	The Disappearing Days	18
3.	A Fancy Dress Affair	25
4.	Princesses Are a Problem	30
5.	The Mystery of the Striped Paint	39
6.	The Unmerciful Music	45
7.	Take a Seat	54
8.	Incrediblanian Summer Time	63
9.	The Birthday Plot	68
10.	The Merry Ministers	76
11.	Someone at the Door	84
12.	Incrediblania Nearly Undone	90

To G. from her little brother

I

The Frantic Phantom

'YOUR Majesty! Your Majesty!' shrieked the Prime Minister of Incrediblania, tearing along the picture gallery and shaking so much that his buttons rattled. 'The palace is haunted! Ghosts, goblins, spectres, banshees, spooks, phantoms, and polterwhatsitsnames!' He collapsed into the arms of the Seventh Footman.

'What's this?' said the King of Incrediblania. 'The palace haunted? Ridiculous! Unheard-of, absurd and most certainly against the rules.'

'N-n-not unheard-of, Majesty,' jabbered the Prime Minister, his teeth chattering in time with his rattling buttons. 'L-l-l-listen!'

From high up in the palace there suddenly arose the most awful and unearthly sound. It wasn't a wail or a cry. It wasn't a yell, hoot, moan, gurgle or scream. It seemed to go right through your ears, down your back and out at your toes. And all your courage went with it.

'Oh, my royal ancestors!' gasped the King, his hair standing up so high his crown hit the ceiling. 'Something must be done about it. Call the C-c-court Magician.'

The Court Magician seemed to be the only one who could listen to the ghastly noise without shivering. 'Mm, it certainly sounds like a ghost, because I can't think what else it sounds like,' he said, when the noise had stopped. 'We must take steps.'

'What's all this about steps?' said a voice, and in came the Queen. 'If it's about dancing, everybody is to wait while I change my shoes.'

'N-n-no, my dear,' said the King. 'It's about a ghost.'

'We must take steps to lay it,' said the Magician.

'You talk about ghosts as if they were linoleum,' said the Queen.

'We must search the palace,' said the Magician. 'We'll each take a different part and if anyone sees anything awful he's to shout.'

'Right!' said the King. The Prime Minister reckoned he didn't have to be told to shout if he saw something awful.

They hunted high and low and middleways. They searched rooms, and looked in cupboards, and behind curtains, and under beds and on top of wardrobes. They found a considerable amount of dust but nothing at all resembling what might be a ghost.

'We'd better stop now,' said the King. 'It's getting dark.'

'Well, that's just the time to see a ghost, if there is one,' said the Queen.

So on went the search. They looked up chimneys and poked down drains, they looked under the carpets and inside the ornaments. They were just going to look behind the pictures, when, *Yow, ow, wah wah wah*, the frightful, awful, terrifying noise broke out again, right overhead, and the search broke up in wild disorder with everyone rushing out screaming almost worse than the haunting noise.

Day after day the search went on, and so, every now and then, did the ghastly noise. It squealed and quavered and blared and twiddled. But nobody could find the ghost. Chiefly because they didn't try very hard in case they did. Anyway nobody could do any searching while the noise was on, as they had to hold both hands over their ears and had none left to search with.

'I can't understand it,' said the King. 'Why should we suddenly start to be haunted now? I mean ghosts don't start haunting just when they think they will. It starts because someone was walled up, or murdered or something.'

'Perhaps it's a rather young ghost,' said the Court Magician, 'who hasn't done any haunting before and is just learning.'

'Well, I wish he'd learn somewhere else,' said the King. Things got awful, they got worse and worse. Several servants left because they couldn't clean for shaking. The Cook found she couldn't make anything but jellies and blancmanges and quivery things like that.

Then one nervous evening, when all was dark and dim, the Seventh Footman, who thought he didn't believe in ghosts, was doing a bit of searching around the attics while everything was quiet. He strode down a murky corridor and flung open a door at the end.

'Ow!' The great, big, strong, fearless footman let out a howl and tore down the corridor, just as the King and the Magician arrived.

'Terrible, ghastly!' yelled the Footman. 'I've seen it! An awful bogey with eyes like plates, and all head and no legs and, ah, ah, ah, ow!'

'Let me see!' cried the Magician. He crept up to the open door, holding his candle high above him.

'Eee! Ow, wow!' he cried. There, sure enough, was a frightful bogey, goggling at him. He slammed the door and rushed back to the others.

One after another footmen and ministers and guards opened the door of the ghastly room and peeped in. But instantly they gave a great shout and fell fainting to the floor, and had to be revived with lemonade. Then along came the Queen, very brisk and busy.

'Now then,' she said. 'What's all this about?'

'P-p-please, Majesty,' quavered the Magician. 'We've found the ghost.' He pointed to the door of the haunted room.

'Let me see this!' cried the Queen, sweeping everybody out of the way. She stalked fiercely to the door and banged on it.

'Who's in there?' she demanded. 'Open, in the King's name, er, I mean the Queen's name,' she said. 'Come out of there at once!'

There was no reply. Not a sound broke the awful stillness except the panting of breath and the chattering of teeth.

'All right then, I shall come and deal with you my own royal self!' declared the Queen.

She flung open the door. Then she gave the most unroyal shriek, louder than anybody had shrieked yet, and went tearing up the corridor.

'Coo!' muttered the others. 'It certainly is a frightful phantom if even the Queen is frightened of it. So what chance have we got of dealing with it?'

Then the King had an idea.

'Let's send for the Royal Fire Brigade,' he said. 'They can climb up their ladders outside the palace and get into the haunted room through the window. Then they can catch the bogey from behind before it sees them. And with their axes and hoses and fire extinguishers and things they ought to be able to settle it pretty quickly.'

So they all went off to the Royal Fire station.

'Well, all right, Your Majesty,' said the Chief of the Fire Brigade. 'But I don't know that we have the equipment for laying ghosts.' He was thinking like mad to find a way of dodging what looked like being a scarey job.

'Yes, you have,' said the Court Magician. 'To exorcize a ghost you simply put it out. If you can put a fire out, you can put a ghost out.'

'But we don't have ghost extinguishers,' protested the Fire Brigade Chief.

'Now, now,' put in the King. 'No arguments, please. Just get up those ladders and exor-thingummy that ghost, or we'll make you redundant.'

So the Fire Brigade put their ladders up outside the haunted room. The firemen drew lots to see who should be first up to deal with the ghost, and wangled it so that the

Chief had to go first. Up the ladder he went, trembling a bit but trying not to show it. With his axe he broke the window and got it open. Then he climbed inside.

Down below the firemen spread a net in case the phantom threw him out. Inside the palace the King, the Magician, and the ministers waited outside the haunted room with bated breath, which is a very uncomfortable thing to wait with.

'I can hear him climbing inside,' said the King. 'Stand back everybody, in case the ghost bursts out!'

Thump, rattle, bump, came some noises from inside the room. Then the door opened.

'Aaaah!' said everyone, getting ready to scream.

But all that happened was that the Fire Brigade Chief stepped out, looking puzzled.

'There's nothing there,' he said. 'At least, no spooks or spectres. Only some old boxes and things.'

The King and the Magician looked at each other in astonishment.

'Perhaps the phantom saw the Fire Chief coming and decided not to wait to be exor-thingummied,' said the King.

But before the Magician could answer, *Waaaaa, boom, shriek, wa-ta-ra*, the ghastly noise started and they all rushed downstairs as fast as they could.

'We shall have to offer a reward to anyone who can get rid of the ghost,' moaned the King, when the noise had stopped again and the Butler had brought in some tea. 'Dear me, this ghost is worse than the dragons we used to be troubled with.'

'Now you be careful, Montgomery,' said the Queen, who had turned up in time for tea as usual. 'Don't you go offering half the kingdom as reward for getting rid of the ghost or we'll be in the same mess we were in over the dragons. And for goodness' sake don't offer the hand of the Princess in marriage, because we've run out of princesses. All three of our daughters are married now.'

'Um, ah, yes, so we have, and they are,' said the King. Then he suddenly thumped the table with his fist.

'So much the better!' he cried. 'What about Egbert Effelfluff – His Royal Highness Prince Egbert? You know, the chap who married our second daughter. He dealt with a couple of dragons and a witch and if he can deal with dragons he can deal with ghosts, and as he's already married to one of our princesses we needn't give him any reward, because he's one of the family.'

'I think that's a bit unfair,' said the Queen, 'taking advantage of relations. But perhaps we could give him a nice present for his trouble.'

So they sent for Prince Egbert and the Princess and told them about the ghosts.

'Psp, psp, psp,' whispered the Princess in Egbert's ear.

'Don't whisper. It isn't polite and it tickles,' said Egbert. But he listened just the same.

'Ha! Oh yes, Majesty Dad,' he said. 'I think we can deal with your frantic phantom all right. Just come upstairs to the haunted room, will you.'

He and the Princess ran upstairs, followed by the King and Queen and the ministers.

'Now, you stay outside,' said the Prince. 'We'll go in and deal with the ghost.'

'I bet they rush out screaming,' said the Magician.

But Egbert and the Princess walked straight into the haunted room and never shrieked a shriek. Instead they picked up something large and rather heavy and brought it out into the passage.

'There's your ghost,' said Egbert, dusting his hands.

'Good gracious!' cried the Queen.

'Well, I'll be whatsnamed!' exclaimed the King.

'Scrambled spells and idiotic incantations!' gasped the Magician.

For the ghastly ghost was nothing more than a big distorting mirror. It was so shaped that it made you look all head and no body or legs. And of course each person who looked at it saw himself. And as his eyes were staring with fright the reflection had staring eyes, only bigger ones. And as his hair was standing on end, the reflection's hair stood on end. But it was all so distorted he didn't recognize himself, and it looked positively frightful. Of course it was dim and murky in the room and the passage, so even with candles you couldn't see very well and nobody had thought of such a thing as a distorting mirror. When the Fire Brigade Chief got in through the window he saw it from the back so he didn't see the awful reflection.

'But how did you know that's what it was?' asked the King.

'We bought it as a surprise side-show for a fair you were going to hold to make money for the kingdom,' said Egbert. 'But you put it off after finding hidden treasure because you didn't need the money. We just put the mirror up here out of the way.'

'Well, thank goodness that's settled the ghost,' said the King later, when he and Egbert and the Court Magician were tidying up the attic and putting the mirror back with its face carefully against the wall.

But there was one thing they had all forgotten. Just then the frightful, wailing, blaring, haunting noise broke out again.

'B-b-but,' stammered the King. 'The noise is coming from higher up. This can't be the haunted room after all!'

'We must have *two* ghosts!' gurgled the Magician, casting spells over himself to make himself unfrightened.

'Oh, no!' cried the King. 'This is too much! Two too much, in fact. Do you think you can deal with this ghost as well, Egbert?'

When the ghostly noise stopped they all went upstairs to the rooms above. The Queen appeared and wanted to know what was going on.

'We've still got to get rid of the other ghost,' said the King.

'What do you mean, the *other* ghost?' demanded the Queen. 'How many of the beastly things have we got? We're positively overrun with them. Anyway, what does this one do?'

'It's the one that makes that awful *tan-ta-ra* noise,' said the King. 'You know . . .'

Before he could finish the Queen said in a rather strange voice, 'Oh! I have an idea for getting rid of the noisy ghost. I wonder I didn't think of it before. All of you go up to the place where the ghost is, at midnight. Don't worry if the noise is noising. Just stuff up your ears. And don't be scared, if you can help it,' she added. 'I shall deal with the ghost.'

'Hm,' said the King to himself. 'We'll have a few guards as well, to be on the safe side.'

That night the terrifying noise began again. It rose high and sank low. It became loud then soft. It gurgled, and bellowed, and moaned, and wailed round the corridors until everyone's hair stood so much on end they couldn't even brush it and certainly didn't try.

Midnight! The strokes of the hour boomed through the palace.

'To the haunted room!' cried the King.

And followed by the Magician, Prince Egbert and the Princess and the guards, he mounted the creaking stairs.

Step by step they climbed, and as they went higher and higher the noise became louder and louder. At last they were outside the door of the attic room from which the sound was coming. It was frightful.

The King rapped on the door. 'Open in the name of the K-k-k-king!' he stuttered.

The door flew open. The King staggered back aghast.

'Good royal gracious!' he gasped. 'Is this the frantic phantom?'

For what do you think they saw there in the haunted attic among the ghastly, ghostly noise?

The Queen herself! And she was playing the trombone. *Tan-ta-ra, tiddley-om-pa, waaa, waaa.* And she was playing it frightfully out of tune and making the most horrifying noises because she had practically no idea how to play it.

Her Majesty put the trombone down and they all laughed for half an hour without stopping.

'I was learning to play this secretly, to give you a nice surprise, seeing how fond you are of music,' she said to the King. 'I never guessed I was your ghost until you said something about the noise going *tan-ta-ra.*'

'Well, if that's your idea of doing something secretly,' said the King, 'I only hope you never try to do something unsecretly. I couldn't stand it. Anyway,' he went on, 'why couldn't you have chosen something nice and lady-like and queenly, such as a harp or a clarinet?'

'Oh,' said the Queen, 'I've always longed to play a trombone. It's such fun sliding that long part in and out.'

So the ghosts of Incrediblania were laid at last. To celebrate it they all had a lovely banquet and the Fire Brigade choir sang *Seventy-Six Trombones* in honour of the occasion.

2

The Disappearing Days

'Oh dear!' groaned the King of Incrediblania. 'Monday again, washing day; the house full of soapy smells and the grounds full of washing. I positively dislike Mondays, and I can't stand washing day!'

'Why not abolish it, Your Majesty?' suggested the Lord Chancellor, who didn't like Monday either, because that was the day he had to put on his heavy wig and elaborate robes and sign no end of documents.

'Hm,' said the King. He looked up 'abolish' in the royal dictionary and found it meant to do away with something and stop having it. 'An excellent idea!' he cried. 'Yes, indeed, we shall abolish Mondays, and with them this horrible, damp, smelly, uncomfortable washing day business.'

He sent for the Astronomer Royal and said, 'It is our royal wish that there shall be no more Mondays in the kingdom of Incrediblania. Kindly abolish them, will you?'

'Ah, now, Majesty,' said the Astronomer Royal. 'And what does Your Majesty, in his wisdom, wish to do with the days that used to be Mondays?'

'Oh!' said the King, who hadn't even thought of that. 'That makes it sort of awkward, doesn't it?'

'It doesn't do anything of the kind,' said the Queen, who had just come in from seeing that the royal washing was pegged out with becoming royal dignity. 'All you have to do is have two Sundays and then go straight on to Tuesday, so the day that was Monday becomes a second

Sunday.' She sat down on the throne feeling delighted because she liked Sundays as she had her breakfast in bed then.

'Yes, of course,' said the King, trying to look as if he had thought of it himself. 'Two Sundays, then go straight on to Tuesday.'

'Very well, Your Majesty,' said the Astronomer Royal, and, drawing his telescope, he was off like the North wind, making all the doors in the palace slam at once.

Presently it was next week. The two Sundays came and went. The Queen had her breakfast in bed two days running, or rather she had her breakfast in bed two days without having to do any running as it wasn't washing day. The church bells went off two days in succession and then it was Tuesday.

'Baskets and Banbury cakes!' roared the King, sniffing the air like a ferocious greyhound. 'What's all this smell of soapsuds? Why is all that washing hanging out in the grounds? I thought I abolished washing day!'

'No, dear,' said the Queen. 'You only abolished Mondays, so washing day has to be on Tuesday now. And why are there only eleven of your hankies in the wash? You used to have twelve.'

'To whatsit with the hankies!' cried the King. 'What's the use of my abolishing Mondays if washing day is going to be on Tuesday?' But the Queen had gone out to count the clothes pegs and didn't hear him.

'Fetch the Astronomer Royal!' shouted the King. 'Tell him to abolish Tuesdays too.'

'And have three Sundays in a row?' asked the Astronomer Royal, when he arrived.

'Well, yes, I suppose so,' said the King, wondering what the Archbishop of Incrediblania would say about all these extra Sundays.

'Three Sundays it shall be, Majesty,' snorted the Astronomer Royal, and he swept off like the West wind, blowing all the royal washing off the lines.

So next week the Queen had breakfast in bed three days in a row. She thought it was exceedingly royal and most enjoyable.

Then came Wednesday, and again the palace was full of soapsud smells and the grounds were full of washing.

'Washing day again, or I'm a piece of stair carpet!' roared the King, ramping round like a caged lion.

'You're nothing so useful,' said the Queen. 'And it *is* washing day even though it is Wednesday.' And she went out to see if the new soap was getting the washing whiter than white as the advertisements said it would.

So the King had another interview with the Astronomer Royal and finished up by telling him to abolish Wednesdays too.

'I'll get rid of these washing days somehow,' he declared.

'This,' said the Queen, having a luxurious breakfast in bed for the fourth day in succession, 'is what I call royal living. I like this abolishing idea. We should do it more often.'

And that, of course, is just what the King found he had to do. Because with Wednesday rubbed out, Thursday became washing day, and when Thursday went the soapsuds and washing in the grounds took place on Friday. And, no sooner had the King got the Astronomer Royal to dispose of Friday, than Saturday was washing day.

'This is ridiculous!' cried the King. 'You're not abolishing these days at all! All you are doing is making the Queen have the washing done one day later each time.'

'Aha, but Majesty,' said the Astronomer Royal craftily, 'I am scientifically assisting Your Majesty to bring about the state of things which Your Majesty desires.'

'Well then, what do you suggest we do?' asked the King.

'Abolish Saturday,' said the Astronomer Royal. 'Her Majesty cannot possibly hold washing day on a Sunday. It isn't done. The Archbishop would never stand for it. It's against the Incrediblanian law to work on Sundays. So if I abolish Saturday that makes it Sunday every day of the week and there can be no washing days at all.'

'Good gracious!' cried the King. 'What an idea! Yes, yes, abolish Saturdays, by all means, and let us have nothing but Sundays.'

'Right,' said the Astronomer Royal, who always had Sunday off and reckoned life was going to be nice and quiet from now on.

'Well, this is what I call being a Queen,' said the Queen, propped up in bed with assorted royal pillows, sipping her tea and feeling exceedingly luxurious. 'Breakfast in bed every day and no washing to worry about. I could go on reigning for ever like this.'

But every day being Sunday didn't turn out quite so jolly as Their Majesties expected. None of the shops ever opened so nobody could buy anything. The trains didn't run, and the buses went only to church and back. And as there was no washing day everything began to get rather grubby. The King couldn't tell whether he was wearing a white shirt, a coloured one or one with stripes, and several times the royal maids laid a rug on the dining table in mistake for a tablecloth.

And the Archbishop of Incrediblania was absolutely worked to death, preaching sermons every day. The clergy were exhausted, and, as people had nowhere to go except to church and nothing to spend their money on, the collections were enormous. They had enough to buy ten new organs and five new cathedrals, but as every day was Sunday they couldn't buy them or get them built. It was terribly frustrating.

'We can't go on like this,' moaned the King. 'We'd better have things back as they used to be; have washing day on Monday and get it over.'

'That would not really be necessary, Majesty,' said the Court Magician. 'I could magic up a royal laundry somewhere nice and remote, say in the middle of the Imperial Forest, and all the washing could be done there and not in the palace at all.'

'A washerama!' cried the Queen, clapping her hands. 'What a lovely idea!'

'Right,' said the King. 'Get on with it at once.'

'Alas, Majesty,' said the Magician, spreading out his hands. 'It is Sunday, and I am not allowed to work on Sundays.'

'Oh, all right,' said the King. 'We'll send for the Astronomer Royal and tell him to put things back as they were. Then you can get on with magicking up the royal laundry.'

'Alas, Majesty,' said the Astronomer Royal, when he was summoned. 'It is Sunday, Your Majesty, and I am not allowed to work on Sundays.'

'Nonsense!' said the Queen. 'You worked on those other Sundays when we were abolishing washing day.'

'Er, no, Majesty, if Majesty will pardon me,' said the Astronomer Royal. 'It was always Monday, Tuesday, Wednesday, and so on, when you ordered me to abolish that day and go straight on to the next one. When I finally abolished Saturdays and made every day Sunday I had to stop work. I can't work again until we get week-days back and I can't bring week-days back without working, so there we are.'

'But-b-b-but,' stammered the King, 'the servants still work every day.'

'Ah, yes, Majesty,' said the Astronomer Royal. 'Domestic servants have always worked on Sundays. There was a special Act of Parliament passed saying that servants should be allowed to work on Sundays in order to get the beds made and the meals laid.'

'Well then,' said the King, 'we shall just have to pass an Act of Parliament saying that the Astronomer Royal may work on Sundays, and then the Astronomer Royal can put the week-days back, so that the Magician can magic up the royal laundry.'

'Alas, Majesty,' said the Prime Minister, when the King told him to call Parliament to pass the new Act. 'Parliament does not meet on Sundays. It is against the law.'

'Oh, oh, oh, we are undone!' moaned the King, clapping his hand to his forehead.

'We are nothing of the kind!' said the Queen, who had had enough of this. 'Listen to me,' she said. 'Astronomer Royal, you are hereby appointed Chief Table Layer to the Royal Household. That makes you a domestic servant and you can work on Sundays. Now, go and lay the dinner, and then put the days back as they were. And you,' she pointed at the Court Magician, 'can then go and produce your royal laundry, and we'll have no more of this nonsense.'

So at last the problem was solved. Incrediblania got its week-days back. The Queen got her royal laundry. The King was free of washing day smells in the palace and the Archbishop went back to preaching only one sermon a week.

But the Astronomer Royal always had to lay the dinner because the King never seemed to get around to abolishing his appointment as Chief Table Layer. Perhaps His Majesty felt there had been a bit too much abolishing done. You can't really blame him.

3

A Fancy Dress Affair

THE King and Queen of Incrediblania had been invited to a very special fancy dress party, and neither of them could think of what to go as.

'It must be something royal and dignified,' said the Queen, 'and something that suits me.' And she flipped over the pages of a fancy dress book. 'So that means I can't go as a pierrot or a gipsy girl, or a Spanish peasant, or a Dutch housemaid, and all the books are full of those sort of dresses.'

'And my costume,' said King, 'mustn't have any sticking-out bits or sharp corners, because they get in the way so. That means I can't go as a pillar-box, or a gas fire, or a teapot, or a grandfather clock, lawn mower, dog kennel, or devil-among-the-tailors. And mine, too, must be royal and dignified, so I can't go as Professor Branestawm, although I'd love to.'

'It's going to be very difficult,' said the Queen. 'I'm going to have forty winks, and then, perhaps, I'll dream about something good.'

So the Queen went to sleep, and the King went out into the garden to see if it would be any good going as a majestic sort of flower.

Just at that moment what should happen but a highly important and frightfully powerful Oriental monarch arrived unexpectedly, to pay a surprise visit to the King and Queen of Incrediblania, whom he had never met but had always wanted to.

'His Extreme Altitude, the Nabob of Nullipop,' an-

nounced the Chief Herald. The Queen, who had only got to her twentieth wink, woke up with a start to find a most decoratively dressed potentate standing before the throne.

'Oh, ah, ha, ha, ha,' she laughed, and clapped her hands. 'Oh, what a lovely idea! However did you think of it?' She thought it was the King with his idea of a fancy dress costume.

'Now, that's royal and dignified, if you like,' she said, picking up the edge of the Nabob's robes and looking at the gold fancy-work on it, while the Nabob put his nose in the air and smiled, thinking she was going to kiss the hem of his gown, a very Oriental sort of compliment where he came from. But, of course, she didn't do anything of the

kind. She flung her arms round his neck and kissed him on the nose instead.

'Oh Monty, you're too perfect,' she said. 'Just like a real Nabob, only more so. Now I can go as a Nabobess or Potentanana or whatever they are called. What a time we'll have!' And grasping the astonished and angry Oriental gentleman round the waist, she waltzed him all round the throne room.

Just then the King came in.

'Heavens!' he cried. Then he grasped the situation with his royal instincts and rushed out again very quietly.

'I, I, I, I, – ' gasped the Nabob, after going three times round the room, his turban half untwisted, one of his slippers kicked off and hanging on a palm tree, and all his several slaves knocking their foreheads on the ground, partly from fear and partly from astonishment. 'How darest thee? Salamanders and swordfish, by the curry of my ancestors, I am annoyed. Stop, s'arrête, avast there, ceasest thee, continuestist notta! Whoa!'

But the Queen only laughed and kept on dancing him, and as the Nabob had used up all the languages he knew except his own, he started shouting out things nobody could understand except his slaves.

'Oh, this outrageous conduct!' thought the Nabob to himself, because he could understand his own language. 'Wait till I get away from this woman. There shall be war, lots of it. Swords and spears and axes all over the place. Everyone shall be cut in little bits several times over. Never have I been treated so, not even by my relations!' He was so annoyed and bursting with rage and indignation that at last he couldn't even understand himself think.

'Your Extremity, Your Extremity! Oh, a thousand apologies doubled, multiplied by themselves and carry one,' cried a voice, and in dashed the King, dressed up to look exactly like the Queen.

'What's this?' demanded the Queen, stopping dancing and letting go of the Nabob. 'Is this me I see, and if so, who am I? Good gracious!'

'Enough!' cried the King, in a very high-pitched voice. 'Away with her to the dungeons! Your Extremity,' he said, 'I humbly apologize. She is the gardener's aunt, masquerading as the Queen. I am the real Queen, and I'm so sorry.'

Then the guards seized the Queen and took her out.

And she didn't resist. You see, she knew there weren't any dungeons, so she couldn't be flung into them, and she recognized the King by a pimple on one ear, and guessed she had rather put her foot in it.

'Pray remain for one moment,' went on the King, still pretending to be the Queen, 'while I fetch His Majesty myself. He will be overjoyed at your coming.' And the Nabob, who wasn't so very overjoyed at his coming himself after what had happened, sat still and said nothing.

Then in came the King dressed in his proper robes, and the Queen trying to look just like the King had looked when he had dressed up as her.

Then the Nabob stood up, and the slaves stopped knocking their heads on the floor.

'Welcome to Incrediblania!' cried the King, and trumpets blew, refreshments were brought in, and people cheered, some of them for the Nabob, but most of them for the refreshments.

'That was a narrow escape,' said the King, after the Nabob had gone. 'You nearly landed us in the most unreasonable war, dancing a potentate about like that.'

'Well, I didn't know he was *really* Oriental silly,' said the Queen. 'I thought he was you until you came in as me. It was all so muddling.'

'Anyway,' said the King, 'it gives me a great idea for the fancy dress ball.'

And what do you think his idea was? Why, the King went as the Queen and the Queen went as the King. They were both as royal and dignified as they thought they ought to be, and they had no end of fun because nobody knew which was which, or even if it was either of them.

But the Queen was very polite to everyone dressed as an Oriental potentate – just in case he really was one.

4

Princesses Are a Problem

BARON Garstleigh and the Duke of Dulstodgy were talking on the steps of the royal palace of Incrediblania when a young man came up, carrying a bunch of flowers and a box of chocolates.

'Excuse me if I appear to pass,' he said. 'I am going to ask the King for the hand of the Princess in marriage.'

'You'll do nothing of the kind!' cried the Duke. 'You keep out of the way. I am going to ask for the hand of the Princess myself.'

'Ho! Are you, then, indeed?' snarled the Baron. 'It's the first I've heard of it, and, let me tell you, it won't work. You will not ask for the hand of the Princess because I intend to marry her myself.'

Of course, they were all three silly six times over, because, although the King had three daughters, which would have been one for each of them, all three Princesses were already married, which left none over for anyone. But they didn't know that. It's a pity they didn't know it, because if they had they would have gone quietly home and kept out of mischief, making models of the royal palace in matchsticks, or collecting glass fire-irons, or something equally harmless. But there you are, the young man was a stranger to Incrediblania, and the Baron and the Duke came from another kingdom where they had heard there was a rich and beautiful princess in Incrediblania, but hadn't heard that she and her two sisters were married. The television wasn't much good in those parts.

But meanwhile they were all getting steaming mad with each other.

'Grrrr!' growled the two noblemen to each other, and both at once to the young man. 'Something must be done about this. We shall see who is going to marry the Princess. Ha!'

'We shall fight, and the winner shall ask for her,' cried the young man.

'No, no, no,' said the others, who were scared of

fighting in case they got hurt. 'Fighting isn't allowed here. We must think of something else.'

'How about an archery contest?' suggested the Baron craftily, because he was mighty hot with a bow and arrow, and felt sure he would win.

'Wonderful idea!' agreed the Duke, who had won prizes for archery, and was absolutely certain *he* would win.

'All right,' said the young man, who didn't draw too mean a bow himself. But he could see the Baron and the Duke were very wily-looking types and he suspected crafty business. So he said, 'There must be a rule that if one of us cheats he must give a bag of gold to each of the others and retire from the contest.'

'Agreed,' said the Baron. And he added artfully, 'If there is any doubt about whether one of us has cheated, if the other two agree that he has then he pays the forfeit.'

'Yes, yes!' shouted the Duke, guessing what the Baron was planning.

'Right!' said the young man.

So they set about arranging an archery contest to see who should ask for the hand of the Princess. The archery targets were set up. The Baron, the Duke and the young man strung their bows, undid their neckties, re-tied their shoelaces and got ready to begin.

The young man took up his position, drew his bow right to the ear and let fly. *Twang!* The arrow landed just inside the gold bullseye on the target.

'Ha!' thought the Baron, reckoning it was going to be a bit of a job to beat that. But he drew his bow and, *ping*, his arrow landed smack in the middle of the gold.

'I've won! I've won!' he cried, throwing his bow into the air.

PRINCESSES ARE A PROBLEM

'Wait a minute, will you?' growled the Duke, as the Baron's bow came down on his hat. 'It's my turn. Not so fast about winning, if you please.'

He drew his bow, took aim and, *ping*, his arrow landed just beside the Baron's.

'You're out!' cried the Duke and the Baron to the young man. 'Now be off, scoot, clear out, make tracks, sling your hook, slope off, vamoose, skedaddle. The Baron and I will now decide the contest between us.'

'Stop!' cried the young man. 'Wait a minute! You cheated, both of you. I saw you. You both stood several paces nearer the target than I did. You were right over the line.'

It was quite true. The nasty noblemen had cheated. They'd done it on purpose.

'I say we didn't cheat!' cried the Baron.

'And I agree with him,' said the Duke. 'And as there are two of us to one of you, according to the rule you made, we did not cheat and you are out of the contest.'

'Yes,' snarled the Baron, which is a mighty difficult word to snarl, but the Baron had had a lot of snarling practice. 'And as you've lost you must hand over a bag of gold. Come on now!' He rubbed his hands together and held them out. 'A lovely bag of jingling, clinking, gorgeous gold. Hand it over!'

But the young man was going to show the nasty nobles they weren't the only ones who could do a bit of clever craftiness.

'Wait a minute!' he cried.

'What, another one?' jeered the Duke. 'That's two minutes you've asked us to wait. If we go on waiting like this we'll all be too old to marry the Princess!'

'You've got the rule all wrong!' cried the young man.

'The rule says if one of us cheats and the other two agree he has cheated he has to pay the forfeit.'

'Of course,' said the others. 'That's what we've done.'

'Oh, no, you haven't,' said the young man. 'You haven't agreed that one of us has cheated. You've agreed that you two didn't cheat. There's nothing about that in the rules.'

The nobles were silent. The young man was quite right.

'Now then,' said the young man, 'you say you haven't cheated. We'll see about that.'

He turned to the Baron. 'Do you agree with me,' he demanded, 'that the Duke cheated and must therefore give each of us a bag of gold and be out of the contest?'

Such a crafty look came over the Baron's face that he began to look like the photo on his passport. 'Wow,' he said to himself. 'This gives me an idea. If I agree with this young man, the Duke will have to give us each a bag of gold, he'll be out of the contest and I shall have only this young man to deal with. Ha ha ha, yes yes, I'll do it!' Then aloud he said to the young man, 'Yes, I do agree that the Duke cheated.'

'What?' screamed the Duke. His socks came down and his hair stood on end with rage. 'You soundrel!' he roared at the Baron. 'You varlet, vagabond, viper, villain! You person of ill repute! How dare you? I protest!'

But it was no use. The rule said that if two of them agreed the third had cheated, that was that. So the dastardly Duke had to hand over a bag of gold to the Baron and the young man.

But the young man hadn't finished with them yet. He turned to the Duke.

'Tell me, Duke,' he said in a very smooth voice, 'do you agree with me that the Baron cheated?'

The Duke pulled his socks up again and smoothed his hair down. He saw a chance to get his bag of gold back from the Baron and get him out of the contest. So he said, 'Yes, yes, I agree, the Baron did cheat.'

'Rogues!' roared the Baron, louder than ever. 'Dishonest persons! Undesirable individuals! Rascals!'

But of course he had to submit and hand over a bag of gold to the young man and one to the Duke. This left the young man with two bags of gold, and the Duke and the Baron one bag of gold each the poorer.

'Right,' said the young man. He packed the gold away in his pockets, unstrung his bow, put on his tie, and picked up the flowers and the box of chocolates. 'Now that you have each agreed, according to the rules, that you cheated, you are both now out of the contest. Good day to you, a merry Christmas when it comes, and I'm sorry I can't raise my hat but, as you see, both hands are occupied.'

'We'll get even with you for this!' shouted the Baron and the Duke. 'We'll tell the King about you! We'll see that you don't marry the Princess!'

But the young man didn't answer. He just marched off to the palace with their gold clinking joyously in his pockets.

'What's all this?' demanded the King, when the young man asked for the hand of the Princess. 'You want to marry the Princess? And what, pray, have you done to deserve such a reward?'

'Pst, pst!' whispered the Queen. 'We haven't got any more princesses. They're all three married, remember?'

'Yes, yes, I know,' whispered the King back, 'but I want to find out if this chap's a genuine hand-of-the-Princess-in-marriage candidate or just a common rascal.

'Now then, as I was saying,' he said to the young man,

'have you rid the kingdom of any phantoms? You can't have done; we haven't any left. Have you slain any dragons, giants, ogres, witches or other undesirable creatures? No, because the kingdom doesn't have any. So why do you come here with a bunch of daisies and a packet of sweets expecting to marry the Princess?'

'Your Majesty,' said the young man, 'allow me to introduce myself, as I do not have an equerry with me to do it for me. I am Don Diabolo de Dumplinge, Prince of Parabolia, Emperor of the Impiric Isles, First Peer of Bunceville, Lord High Elevation of the Horizontal Mountains, and here is the address of my kingdom from which you can obtain a free illustrated booklet with full details by sending a stamped addressed envelope.'

The King looked at the Queen, who said, 'He seems a nice, personable sort of young man.'

'Yes, indeed,' said the King. 'But how can we give him the hand of the Princess in marriage when we've run out of princesses? We can't just order another one.'

'Well, it does seem a pity to waste him,' said the Queen. 'I've taken quite a fancy to him and he'd come in very handy to balance things up on State Occasions. I mean, our three daughters and their husbands don't even out very well. There are two couples on one side of us, and only one on the other. If we . . .'

'Yes, yes, I know,' said the King impatiently. 'But as we haven't got another princess it can't be done.'

'What about Cousin Connie's girl?' said the Queen. 'You know, the pretty, fair one, who makes such delicious sponge sandwiches.'

'What about her?' said the King. 'She may be a good cook but she isn't a princess, neither is she our daughter.'

'No, dear,' said the Queen, 'but she could be. We just

adopt her by royal proclamation and she becomes Princess Poppy of Incrediblania and our fourth daughter, both at once.'

'Wonderful!' said the King, and, not bothering to ask the young man whether he liked delicious sponge sandwiches, but assuming that he liked pretty, fair princesses, he said, 'Kindly go and sit in the waiting room, while we get a princess for you.'

But it wasn't going to be as easy as that because Cousin Connie had three daughters, and the two elder ones were frightfully fierce, bossy dames, and they both insisted they ought to have first pick when it came to imported husbands.

'Oh dear!' said the King. 'We don't want to adopt those two. They'll have the whole place reorganized and twenty-five awkward rules set up, so that we shan't be able to do as we like in our own palace.'

'We must find husbands for them,' said the Queen. 'Perhaps Don Thingummy has a few spare brothers.'

The Prince was a one and only, but he did see a neat way of ensuring that the Duke and the Baron couldn't go making trouble for him as they had threatened. He told the King about them, and how they were going to ask for the hand of the Princess. And the King promptly sent guards out to collect them.

'We have done no wrong!' protested the nasty nobles. 'He cheated us.' They pointed at the Prince. 'He did us in at artful archery. It is he who should be arrested.'

'Pah!' snorted the King. 'You are not arrested. You are not charged with anything. You were coming here to ask for the hand of the Princess in marriage, weren't you?'

'Er, er, er, yes, Majesty!' stuttered the nobles.

'Right!' said the King. 'Then here you are. Let the ladies be brought in!' he cried.

'Now,' said the King. 'These ladies are not princesses, but then you are not princes, so you are not entitled to marry princesses. But they'll make very excellent wives for you, I'm sure.'

Then in swept Cousin Connie's two elder daughters who gave shrieks of delight at the sight of the nobles, marched them off to the cathedral, married them, ticked them off for wearing the wrong coloured shirts and had them doing as they were told in no time.

'Well,' said the King, 'we've certainly managed to cancel out two rascally nobles and two awkward ladies very neatly, at one go.'

'And got ourselves a nice new son-in-law as well,' beamed the Queen, patting the Prince on the shoulder.

'Not to mention a charming new daughter,' said the King, kissing Princess Poppy. 'You know,' he said, 'people are always saying that when your daughter gets married you aren't so much losing a daughter as gaining a son. But this time we are gaining not only a son but an extra daughter too.'

'And delicious sponge sandwich for tea!' mumured the Queen, who was rather a one for delicious things to eat.

5

The Mystery of the Striped Paint

'THERE is something,' said the Queen, 'that I want very much, cannot possibly do without and intend to have.'

'Yes, my dear,' said the King, knowing it was almost certainly going to be something he could not afford.

'I like stripes,' said the Queen. 'They're the in thing. They're absolutely way out.'

'How can they be in if they're way out?' thought the King, but he knew better than to say it.

'Well,' went on the Queen. 'What I want is some nice striped paint to have the summer house painted with. It will make us the envy of all the surrounding kingdoms. The Queen of Farrawania will be absolutely emerald green with envy. And besides,' she added, 'don't forget His Extreme Altitude the Nabob of Nullipop is coming to pay a second visit to us. These Oriental gentlemen are mad about stripes. They have their palace domes done over with them, they wear striped clothes, they eat striped food . . .'

'And they talk striped language, if I remember,' said the King.

'Now, now,' said the Queen. 'Have some striped paint ordered to have the summer house painted with when his Extremity gets here. He's in a bit of an Eastern temper just now because our royal coach scraped a bit of marzipan-looking decoration off his carriage the other day and I want to smooth him down a bit before he starts declaring wars.'

'Were you driving the royal coach at the time?' asked

the King, who knew the Queen was rather given to getting the royal coachman to let her drive, and was also given to running into things when she did. Usually expensive things. And he reckoned this was really why the Queen was so keen on having striped paint for the summer house.

'Well, yes, I may have been driving it just a little bit,' said the Queen. 'But never mind that. Order the striped paint. I've promised the Nabob he shall see our summer house being painted with striped paint, and we don't want to upset him again, especially after that time I thought he was you in fancy dress and made him dance round the throne room.'

'But there isn't any striped paint,' said the King.

'Nonsense,' said the Queen. 'Fetch the royal painters!'

But when the Royal Painters and Imperial Decorators and Majestic Varnishers were all lined up in front of the throne they all said the same thing – that there wasn't any striped paint. It didn't exist.

'Stuff and nonsense!' snapped the Queen. 'I've seen some myself. The barber's pole up the street is painted with it.'

'But, my dear –' protested the King.

'I won't hear another word of your silly excuses,' said the Queen. 'I'm going to stay for a week with Cousin Connie, but I'll be back on Saturday in time for the Nabob's arrival, and, if there isn't some striped paint for the summer house when I get back, somebody's going to lose his head!' And she looked very hard at the Lord Chief Painter and Decorator, whose face immediately went white as whitewash with fright.

'Dear, dear, this is most upsetting,' said the King, when Her Majesty had gone. 'Striped paint doesn't exist, so we can't get any, and, if we don't get any, half the painters

THE MYSTERY OF THE STRIPED PAINT 41

will be dismissed, and that means I shall have to climb up on ladders and paint the palace this spring. And, worst of all, the Nabob of Nullipop will get all annoyed when he can't watch the summer house being painted in stripes and start declaring wars. Oh dear, oh dear!'

Then everyone started thinking away like anything to try to find out what they could do about it. They thought and thought for days and days. Monday went by, and Tuesday, and Wednesday, but nobody had thought how to get any striped paint.

'Oh dear, there goes Thursday,' said the King the next day, 'and nothing thought of.'

And everybody pulled themselves together and thought twice as hard as before, while Friday went whizzing past, and seventeen of the thinkers had brain fever and the rest frightful headaches with thinking so hard.

'Stop!' roared the King at last, suddenly leaping off the throne. 'I have thought of what to do.'

He rushed the royal painters and decorators and people into the garden to the summer house, and whispered and pointed and waved his hands about until they all understood his great idea.

Saturday arrived, and so did the Queen, and so did the Nabob. First of all the King made everyone sit down and have a large tea, and they talked about the weather, and the price of food, and how unsatisfactory tradesmen were, and how the Queen's cat wouldn't eat anything but sardines. And all the time the royal painters were hard at work doing mysterious things to the summer house.

'Now, what about this striped painting for the summer house?' said the Queen, suddenly remembering about it herself.

'Yes, my dear,' said the King, having a look out of the

window to see that everything was ready. 'It was awfully difficult, but we have got some striped paint.'

They all went outside to the summer house, where the painters were standing in a row. And, as the Nabob came out, they all saluted him with their brushes which pleased him very much.

'You may now paint the summer house with striped paint,' said the Queen graciously.

Then, *flip flop*, went the brushes, and sure enough the painters were painting the summer house in stripes.

'Lovely!' cried the Queen, when it was all done. 'I knew you could find some striped paint if you tried.'

But how could it be? There simply isn't any striped paint. Paint has to be the same colour all over. Yet the royal painters had painted the summer house in stripes right in front of the Queen's eyes. And they hadn't done it by painting the stripes with different coloured paint. That would have taken too long. No, the royal painters had just painted the paint on like any ordinary paint and it had come out in stripes of different colours. Impossible. But it happened.

It was the King's great idea. First of all, while the Queen was away, he had told the royal painters to paint the summer house in pretty coloured stripes, using ordinary coloured paint. It was a long job but they just got it finished and the paint dry a second or so before the Queen arrived back. Then, while the tea was still raging, the royal painters painted the summer house all over with whitewash. Yes, ordinary whitewash.

Then, while the Queen was watching the painters paint the summer house with striped paint, all they did was paint it with clean water. And of course, they simply painted off all the whitewash and left the stripes showing.

His Extreme Altitude the Nabob of Nullipop was so delighted that the King and Queen had had the royal summer house painted in stripes in his honour that he completely forgave the Queen for chipping a bit off his carriage and gave her a lovely string of jewels. Striped ones.

'They look like bullseyes,' murmured the King.

'I think they're in very good taste,' said the Queen, who liked the taste of anything sweet.

'Well,' said the King to the Lord Chief Painter afterwards. 'At least we'll know how to make it look as if we've invented spotted paint or even flowered paint if the Queen should want any.'

But thank goodness she didn't, which saved a lot of trouble and a tremendous amount of whitewash.

6

The Unmerciful Music

'LA da da, tra la di!' The King of Incrediblania was singing in his bath. He was very fond of music, was the King; or at least he was fond of what he thought was music, which wasn't always the same thing. He came down to breakfast whistling one of his favourite tunes and cracked his egg like someone playing the drum.

'Good morning, good morning, good morning!' he sang to the Queen, who had already begun and was starting on the royal marmalade. 'You know, my dear, I think it's time we had a royal orchestra. I've thought so ever since you showed how fond of music you were by trying to learn the trombone, and made us think the palace was haunted.'

'Eat the top of your egg before it gets cold,' said the Queen, who still felt a bit red round the ears about her trombone playing.

'All the ministers could be in it,' said the King, meaning, of course, the orchestra, not the top of his egg.

'Pass the butter, please,' said the Queen, changing the subject again.

'And learn to play different instruments,' replied the King, changing it back.

'The man from the royal laundry will be here in a minute,' said the Queen.

'And, of course, I shall conduct them,' went on the King.

Just then there was a ring at the door and the Queen shot out, hoping it was the laundry. But the King went on cutting the crusts off his toast, which he liked to do because he had weak teeth, but which the Queen didn't let him do because she thought the crusts would make his hair curl.

'We shall have the first practice next Monday,' said the King. 'Everyone who has an instrument is to bring it, and I will get some for the others.' And off he went while the Queen was hunting all over the palace for his twelve hankies to send to the royal laundry.

The King had a slight bother getting the royal orchestra organized because some of the ministers couldn't play anything unless it had a handle to turn; while some of them were so nervous of offending the King that they said they could play this and that and made up their minds to learn quickly. But others decided not to learn at all, because they guessed the King wouldn't know by the noise they made whether they could play or not.

But the Prime Minister could play the mouth organ. The Lord Chief Justice was good at imitating musical instruments. And the Lord Chancellor could whistle through his teeth, and, though he could whistle only one note, he whistled that extremely well.

Every day the royal orchestra practised hard. And every day the noise it made grew more fearsome but no more tuneful. The Lord Chief Justice, who had been given the Queen's trombone, as she didn't want it any more, simply pushed it in and out and imitated a trombone with his mouth. The Lord Chancellor whistled his one note and kept it up without stopping except for breath. The others were blowing and puffing and scraping and banging, according to what kind of instruments they were trying to play.

'This is awful!' groaned the Queen. 'Now I know why

they thought the palace was haunted when I was trying to play the trombone. But at least there was only one of me.'

She kept begging the King to stop, but all he said was, 'One has to learn to make an awful noise before one can play music. You ought to know that, my dear. Remember when you were trying to play the trombone.'

And on he went, urging the royal orchestra to still greater efforts.

'I simply must stop this terrible row!' gasped Her Majesty. 'But how can I do it?'

Then her eye fell on her work basket which was full of coloured balls of wool left over from the jumpers she had made for her favourite nieces.

'Ha, yes! That's what I shall do!' she said to herself.

That night, while the King and ministers were asleep, the Queen crept secretly to the band room with her basket of balls of coloured wool. She stuffed them into as many of the instruments as she could. They wouldn't stuff into the Prime Minister's mouth organ, of course. But she packed all the trombones and trumpets and saxophones as tight as they would go.

Next day the King announced that he would hold a Grand Festival of Music in the palace grounds, to which everyone was invited. And the heralds, who had to make the announcement, added a bit about free refreshments, because they didn't think anyone would come just to listen to the frightful music. So the royal lawn was absolutely crowded, and the King was delighted.

'Ladies and Gentlemen!' he said. 'We shall begin by playing the Consternatio in K and a half sharp minor, by Flookempusha."

He raised his stick and began to conduct.

'*Zim, zimmy, wa, wa!*' went the Prime Minister on his mouth organ.

'*Yan to ra ra wa wa ra!*' went the Lord Chief Justice, doing his trombone imitation.

'*Wheeeeeee!*' whistled the Lord Chancellor.

But not another sound came from the orchestra. The balls of wool the Queen had stuffed into the instruments prevented the slightest sound coming out.

'Stop!' cried the King. 'What's the matter? We've practised this enough! Now play!' He raised his stick and brought it down again, but, though the ministers blew and puffed till their eyes came out on stalks, not a sound came from the stuffed-up instruments.

His Majesty looked at the crowd. Some who thought the concert was over began to applaud.

But the King wasn't going to be beaten.

'Play, or off with your heads!' he hissed. 'This is your last chance!'

He raised his stick. The ministers took such enormous breaths they burst buttons off important places. Then all of a sudden out shot all the coloured balls of wool, high in the air, over the hedge and down in a shower into the next-door kingdom of Farrawania.

Then on went the unmerciful music at double full blast. The Consternatio in K and a half sharp minor finished with a quadruple forte crash that sounded as if all the stars in the sky had collapsed together into a tank full of glass saucers. And the King bowed, and the crowd all went rushing in for the refreshments.

The Court Magician of the neighbouring kingdom of Farrawania was being given a telling-off by the Queen of that kingdom.

'You call yourself a Magician,' she snorted, 'but you

can't magish a bit! Unless you do some noticeable magic this minute, off with your head! And see if you can magic that on again.'

'I can make an egg disappear,' wailed the Magician.

'I've watched eggs disappear till I'm dizzy!' said the Queen. 'Why don't you wave your hands and produce something pretty out of the air?'

'I, I, I – ' began the Magician, who knew jolly well he could wave his hands clean off and never produce anything by doing it.

'Do as I say!' commanded the Queen. 'Wave your hands.'

Helplessly the Magician raised his long, skinny hands. Wearily he waved them in the air. Desperately he mumbled a spell.

And down came a shower of bright-coloured balls of wool.

The Magician gaped.

'There, I knew you could do it if you tried!' snapped the Queen. And off she went, not guessing that the balls of wool had come from the instruments of the royal orchestra of Incrediblania next door. She even thought the frightful noise the orchestra was making was all part of the Magician's magic.

Some time later the Queen of Farrawania was having tea with the Queen of Incrediblania.

'My dear,' said the Queen of Farrawania, 'you know that Court Magician of ours?'

'Oh, don't I?' said the Queen of Incrediblania. 'Those awful disappearing eggs!'

'Of course,' said the Queen of Farrawania, starting on her seventh cake, 'I simply couldn't stand it any longer. So I said he must do some better magic or off with his head. You know I was never a one to mince my words. I pointed out how silly he was. Told him to wave his hands and produce something pretty from the air. And, my dear, he did it!'

'No?' whispered the Queen of Incrediblania.

'Yes, he simply did!' said the other Queen. 'Waved those long skinny hands of his and down came coloured balls of wool all over the place . . . what's the matter?'

The Queen of Incrediblania had suddenly burst out laughing in the middle of an éclair, and she nearly choked.

'Was this last Wednesday afternoon?' she asked, when she had recovered, 'because if it was, ha ha ha, oh dear!'

But suddenly an idea occurred to the Queen of Incrediblania. Here, she thought, was a chance to stop the King's frightful orchestra really and truly, for, of course, the balls of wool hadn't stopped it as they had been blown out. So Her Majesty didn't say a thing about why everything was so funny, and left the Queen of Farrawania feeling as if she were going to come to the boil with curiosity.

'I know all about your balls of wool from the sky,' said the Queen of Incrediblania to the Court Magician of Farrawania. And she told him what really had happened about his magic.

'Oh dear!' wailed the Magician. 'And I really thought I had done a proper magic at last.'

'Well, nobody need know you haven't,' said the Queen of Incrediblania. 'I won't say a word about it, on one condition.'

'What's that?' moaned the Magician, guessing it was going to be a horribly hard condition.

'That you put a magic of some kind on the royal orchestra of Incrediblania,' said the Queen, 'and stop it from playing. I don't care whether it's a real magic or a conjuring magic, as long as it stops the orchestra from playing. But if you don't do it, I'll tell your Queen what a fraud you are.'

'All right, Majesty,' agreed the Magician. But how he was going to magic the Royal Orchestra of Incrediblania into not playing any more was considerably more than he could think of.

In three days' time the King of Incrediblania was bringing his orchestra to Farrawania. For two days and two nights the Magician tried to think how to magic the orchestra. Then he stopped thinking at all, and was immediately hit with an astonishing idea.

Hurriedly he made some secret preparations and had just finished them when the King and Queen of Incrediblania arrived, accompanied by the orchestra, all in their best clothes.

'We're simply longing to hear your wonderful orchestra,' gushed the Queen of Farrawania, while the Queen of Incrediblania stuffed her handkerchief into her mouth to stop herself laughing.

Then they all went along for refreshments and that gave the Magician a chance to work his dastardly idea.

Presently everyone was as full of refreshments as politeness would let them be, except the King of Incrediblania, who was only as full as the Queen would let him be.

The ministers picked up their instruments and the King of Incrediblania picked up his conducting stick.

'We shall play the January February March!' he announced.

Down came the stick. Out went the ministers' cheeks. But oh ho, out didn't come any music.

'Don't say the Magician has really done it!' thought the Queen of Incrediblania.

Suddenly, with a *whoosh*, out from nearly all the instruments came a cloud of something.

'Ooosh!' gasped the King. 'Ah-h-h-h-h-tishoooo! Tishooooo! Tishoooo!'

The Magician of Farrawania had filled the instruments of the King's orchestra with pepper. And it had blown into the King's face. He sneezed and sneezed, and couldn't even stop for meals.

Was that what the Magician called a magic? It certainly was. Not much of a magic, but most definitely a way of stopping the King's orchestra from playing, because the King had had enough.

'I think, ahtishoooo,' he sneezed, 'we had better get a record player instead of an orchestra. It, ahtishooo, seems safer.'

'Lovely!' cried the Queen, and she bought the most expensive record player the kingdom could provide. It had five turntables and ten loud-speakers and rows and rows of buttons to play about with. And she bought all her favourite records, but not the January February March, or the Consternatio in K and a half sharp minor.

So that was the end of the royal orchestra of Incrediblania. And the Lord Chief Justice was able to give up imitating a trombone and imitate a Lord Chief Justice instead, which he didn't do so well, but never mind.

7
Take a Seat

SPRING was taking place in Incrediblania, complete with flowers, singing birds, sunshine and sprouting trees.

And to commemorate this exciting event, all the seats in the palace gardens had been newly painted.

Mr Joshua Jellijorge knew all about the spring and the flowers and the birds and the trees. But he didn't know about the newly painted seats in the royal gardens. How could he? He didn't even know he was walking into the royal palace gardens because the gate had been taken away to be painted, and the severe inscription *Royal Gardens, Private, Keep Out. No Admittance. Entry Forbidden. Go Away!* had been taken away to be newly painted too. So along he strolled, all innocent and enjoying the scenery, and sat down on one of the newly painted seats. Then he popped a toffee into his mouth and settled down to enjoy things.

He was half-way through his fourth chew when who should come majestically along but the Queen herself. She stopped, she rubbed her eyes. She didn't believe what she saw. There was Mr Joshua Jellijorge calmly sitting on a royal seat in the most private and severely forbidden palace gardens.

And worse than that, he didn't stand up when the Queen came along. He couldn't. He was stuck fast to the wet paint.

'Now, now, now, now!' said the Queen, in a voice that shrivelled up a whole row of daffodils. 'What's this, may I

TAKE A SEAT

ask? Who are you and why do you not stand up when the Queen passes?'

But Joshua couldn't answer any more than he could stand up. He was just as stuck up with the toffee in his mouth as he was stuck down with the wet paint on the seat.

'Ha!' snorted the Queen. 'So you have the impudence to come here into the private palace gardens, sit yourself on a seat, refuse to stand up when the Queen passes, and you do not even have the good manners to reply to a civil question.'

'Glug!' said Joshua, which was all he could get out through the toffee.

'We can't have this,' said the Queen. 'Guards!' she called.

'Yes, Majesty?' said the Captain of the Guard, saluting, clicking his heels, and bowing all at once.

'What shall we do with this, er, this, er – '

'Miscreant, Majesty?' suggested the Captain.

'Yes,' said the Queen. 'What shall we do with him to punish him for sitting on seats in the royal gardens?'

'How about flinging him into the dungeons, Majesty?' suggested the Captain.

'Nonsense!' snapped the Queen. 'We haven't any dungeons.'

'But we have, Majesty!' said the Captain. 'The new dungeons Your Majesties ordered are now finished and all ready with hideous curtains, frightful furniture and terrifying pictures on the walls. All they need is someone to be flung into them.'

'Splendid!' cried the Queen. 'We shall be graciously pleased to celebrate the opening of the new dungeons by having this miscreant flung into them.' And off she went.

'Come on now!' said the Captain of the Guard to Joshua. 'We've got to fling you into the dungeons. Stand up and be flung.'

But of course Joshua couldn't stand up, and he couldn't explain why.

The guards got hold of him and tried to get him off the seat but he was stuck so fast they couldn't move him.

'We shall have to fling the seat in with him,' said the Captain of the Guard.

'Her Majesty didn't say anything about flinging the seat into the dungeons,' said the Assistant Captain.

'Well, she didn't say we weren't to fling it in,' said the Captain. So, with a great deal of 'A bit more to me!' and 'Easy there!' and 'Mind the tulips!', Joshua Jellijorge and the seat were flung carefully into the dungeons.

A little later on the King came strolling along with a copy of the *Incrediblania Gazette* to read all about how he had launched the new Incrediblanian submarine.

'Ah,' he said, 'I'll just sit on my favourite seat by the daffodils while I read about me.'

But the seat wasn't there. It had been flung into the dungeon with Mr Joshua Jellijorge stuck to it.

'Ho there!' he called to the Keeper of the Royal Gardens. 'There used to be a seat here and it's been taken away. Have it put back at once!' And he stamped into the palace, determined to have an extra lump of sugar in his morning coffee to make up for it.

'If the seat goes back into the gardens, this chap will have to go back with it,' said the Captain of the Guard, when the Keeper of the Royal Gardens told him what the King had said.

'Well, orders is orders,' said the Keeper of the Royal Gardens.

'The King must be obeyed,' agreed the Captain of the Guard. And with a lot of heaving, and pushing, and lifting, and shouting of 'To me! From you! Easy does it!' the seat was put back into the palace gardens with Joshua still stuck to it.

After lunch the Queen went for a walk in the palace gardens to stop herself getting too fat. And she came upon Joshua sitting still stuck to the seat that the guards had brought back.

And again Joshua didn't get up because he couldn't.

'Guards!' roared the Queen, and she spoke off a whole lecture at Joshua so fast and furious that he didn't get a chance to say anything.

'Fling this, er, er,' she said.

'Miscreant, Majesty?' suggested the guards.

'Yes, fling this miscreant into the dungeons again.'

'Her Majesty didn't say anything about flinging the seat in too,' said the Assistant Captain.

'Oh, bother it!' snapped the Captain. 'If he's flung, it's flung!' And back into the dungeons Joshua went, seat and all.

But, oh dear, presently along came the King just ready

for a nice sit-down after lunch. And again his favourite seat wasn't there.

'Didn't I say the seat was to be put back here?' he cried to the Keeper of the Royal Gardens.

'Er, yes, Majesty, but Majesty –' stammered the Keeper.

'Have the seat brought back again at once!' cried the King, and he went back to the palace to have a rest in his favourite armchair.

'If the seat goes back, he goes back too!' said the Captain of the Guard. So back went Joshua once again, still stuck to the seat, but not saying anything even though he hadn't got any toffee left to stick his jaws up; because he didn't think anything he could say would do much good.

Then along came the Queen, looking for some flowers to cut for the royal tea table. And when she saw Joshua sitting there again she was ready to explode.

'To the dungeons with him!' she cried.

So back went Joshua and the seat once more.

And every time the King came along and saw the seat wasn't there he ordered it back. And every time the Queen came along and saw Joshua on the seat she ordered him into the dungeons. The guards were getting worn out flinging Joshua and the seat about. Joshua got so dizzy he didn't know whether he was coming or going.

Sometimes the King and Queen would come along so quickly after each other that the guards didn't have time to finish flinging Joshua into the dungeons before they had to fling him out again and get the seat back into the palace garden.

'Oh dear, this is awful!' moaned the Captain of the

Guard. 'Her Majesty gave fifteen flinging orders and I don't think we've flung him more than twelve times. That makes us three flingings behind.'

Poor Joshua still couldn't say a word in protest because he was so dizzy being flung in and out of the dungeons.

At last the Queen happened to pass by just as the guards had put Joshua and the seat back in the palace garden and were about to fling him into the dungeons again.

'Enough of this!' cried the Queen, meaning enough of her finding Joshua sitting on the seat, but the guards thought she meant enough of flinging him into the dungeons.

'Yes, Majesty!' gasped the Captain, very out of breath.

'I will *not* have this person sitting in the palace gardens!' said Her Majesty. 'Have him brought before the King and me this afternoon.' And she swept on.

The Captain of the Guard stared after her with his eyes spinning round.

'If we bring this chap before the King and Queen,' he said, 'we'll have to bring the seat too. But Her Majesty didn't say anything about bringing the seat.'

'Well, orders are orders,' said the Assistant Captain. And so the guards staggered into the throne room, carrying the seat with Joshua Jellijorge still stuck to it.

'Now now, what's all this?' exclaimed the King. 'How dare you bring garden seats into the throne room?'

'And how dare you keep sitting down in our royal presence?' cried the Queen, fixing Joshua with a fierce look.

'P-p-p-p-p-please, Majesty,' stammered Joshua. 'I'm stuck to the seat. The paint was wet when I sat on it.'

'Indeed?' cried the Queen. 'And why did you sit on a

TAKE A SEAT

seat in the palace gardens? Don't you know it is forbidden?'

'Please, Majesty, I didn't know it was the palace gardens,' said Joshua.

'The gate to the gardens has been taken away to be painted,' said the Captain of the Guard. 'So he didn't know he was going into the forbidden royal gardens where no admission is allowed and keeping out is compulsory according to Act of Parliament number...'

But the Queen began to giggle.

'Oh dear!' she said, 'Oh, ha ha, ha ha! It really is funny, you know, if you look at it the right way.'

'Ha, ha, ha,' said Joshua, wondering which way to look at being stuck to a seat and flung rapidly in and out of dungeons, for it to be funny.

'Er, um,' said the King. 'I really think we owe this gentleman an apology. We should have put a temporary notice at the entrance to the palace gardens.'

'And a *Wet Paint* notice on the seat,' said the Queen, who could never resist touching painted things that had a *Wet Paint* notice on them, to see if it really meant it.

'Well, now,' said the King. 'I think we must be just and make some amends to this gentleman. We therefore command that it is our royal pleasure,' he said, 'that every effort shall be made to remove him from the seat, or the seat from him whichever is the less difficult. And then we shall appoint you,' he looked at Joshua, 'to be Royal Keeper of Wet Paint Notices, so that nobody shall ever again get stuck on a seat in the palace gardens, and be flung in and out of dungeons.'

'We had better also award him a new pair of trousers,' said the Queen.

'Indeed, yes. In fact, a whole new suit,' added the King.

'In green velvet with a yellow waistcoat?' asked Joshua, who always wanted a suit like that but couldn't afford it.

'Certainly,' said the King. 'And a good tea with crumpets, three kinds of bread and butter, eight kinds of fancy cakes, and oodles of cream, to make up for things.'

So Joshua was carried off laughing and shaking hands with himself, to be suitably compensated for being so stuck up as to pinch the King's seat. And the brand new royal dungeons were empty once more, all ready to have someone else flung into them, next flinging time.

8

Incrediblanian Summer Time

'SOMETHING called Summer Time starts in a place called England tomorrow,' said the King of Incrediblania, opening the morning paper and getting all tangled up in it.

'Does it?' said the Queen. 'Give me the page with the cookery recipes before you lose it.'

'I think we ought to have some summer time here,' said the King, who liked sitting out in the sun and thinking, and liked better still just sitting out in the sun. 'All we have to do is put the clocks an hour fast and it doesn't get dark so soon.'

'You'd better leave the clocks alone,' said the Queen. 'The last time you did anything to the clock you had three pieces left over when you put it together again, and now it strikes seven at ten past five.'

'Never mind,' said the King. 'I shan't have to take it to bits this time; just put it forward an hour.'

'Incrediblanian Summer Time starts tomorrow,' said the King, ringing for the Butler. 'The clock will be put forward one hour.'

'Yes, Majesty,' said the Butler. And, as soon as everyone had gone to bed, he put the palace clock forward one hour, in case he didn't remember in the morning.

Next morning the King woke up and remembered about the Summer Time.

'Ha!' he said. 'Better put the clock forward. Nobody else will remember to do it.' So down he went in his royal pyjamas and put the clock on an hour, just missing the

Queen who had already been down and put it on an hour herself, as she didn't trust the servants to do it properly. So that made it three hours fast altogether.

Then, while the royal family were getting dressed and coming down, the Cook popped out and put it an hour fast herself, because she had to get meals by it, and wasn't leaving anything to chance. And she had no sooner gone than the Lord Chamberlain, who considered himself responsible for everything connected with the royal house-

INCREDIBLANIAN SUMMER TIME

hold, came in and put it another hour fast. This meant that five people had put the clock an hour fast each, but none of them knew the other had done it.

'Their Majesties are late with breakfast this morning,' said the Butler, as he carried the last of the empty dishes to the kitchen. 'It must be that daylight saving. Why, it's past lunch-time already.'

'Yes,' said the Cook, 'I never did hold with those foreign ideas. You'd better go back and lay the lunch now, or they won't have time for it before tea.'

So back went the Butler, and the King and Queen had lunch straight on from breakfast as if it was one enormous meal.

'If this happens when you have Summer Time,' said the King, between the mouthfuls, 'I vote we have it always.'

Then, while they were having lunch, the man who looked after the clocks came in with instructions from the Prime Minister that the King wanted the palace clock put forward an hour. So he put it forward, but the Prime Minister popped in just afterwards and put it forward again, because he was afraid the man would forget. But the man hadn't forgotten, neither had his assistant, who also came in and put the clocks an hour fast to make sure, not knowing it had been done lots of times already. So the royal family had hardly time to finish their breakfast-lunch before it was time for tea.

'They must be an awfully hungry lot in those foreign places,' said the Queen, doing her best with a jam tart and a cup of tea.

'I expect it's having sea all round them that gives them an appetite,' said the King.

But even then they hadn't finished, for during tea the Queen's personal maid had put the clock on an hour because she had heard the Queen talk about it and wanted to please her. And the King's valet did the same thing. So did the two page-boys. So dinner was served in the middle of tea in order to get it in time.

'Now I know what people mean when they say life is all meals,' grumbled the Cook, who had been having a terrible time in the kitchen trying to get all the meals ready at once to keep up with the clock.

By this time the clock was exactly twelve hours fast, so that it looked as if it was midnight although it was really only mid-day.

'It's a wonderful thing, this Summer Time,' said the King. 'Now we can call Incrediblania the kingdom on which the sun never sets.'

Then time went on and on and on, and still it didn't get dark.

'This is the funniest day I ever spent,' said the King. 'I'd no idea it would be like this when I put the clock on an hour.'

'You put the clock on an hour?' cried the Queen. 'Why, so did I!'

'And I!' cried the Lord Chamberlain and the Prime minister both at once.

'And I, Majesties!' said the Butler, the Cook, who had just come in for orders, and the two page-boys.

'Heavens!' cried the King. 'We must be living in tomorrow, and what shall we do when we get there and there isn't any of it?'

'If that means we start meals over again, I'm leaving,' thought the Cook. But just then the King jumped up as everyone was making a rush for the clock.

'Stop!' he cried, and they all stopped, except the clock.

'If we all go putting the clock back we shall be starting

yesterday over again!' cried the King, who had had toothache yesterday and didn't want it again. 'Everyone stay still while I do it myself. What's the right time?' he asked.

Just then the clock struck seven.

'That means it's ten past five,' said the Queen. 'It always does that since you took it to bits.'

'Then it's right,' said the King. And, of course, it was, because a clock twelve hours fast tells the same time as a clock not fast at all.

'Anyone who wants Summer Time after this,' said the King, 'can go abroad for it.' And everyone said, 'Hear, hear!' But they didn't go.

9

The Birthday Plot

CHEERING, rejoicing, flag-waving and hat throwing-up were happening in the kingdom of Incrediblania, for it was about to be the King's birthday. Banquets were going to occur, feasting and dancing and illuminations would take place. And the great happening of the celebrations was to be a royal salute of twenty-one guns firing roses over the King and Queen as they came out on the palace balcony. It was going to be a great day. No wonder everybody was pleased and excited.

Everybody? Well, no, not the cunning Count Bakwerdz, who hated the King, and was always planning mischief against him. Twice the Count had been caught, and his plots unmasked. Twice he had been flung into prison but each time the King had forgiven him. He had let him have luxuries in prison and finally let him out of prison as long as he promised to behave.

But the crafty Count didn't keep his promises, and now, in his grim, grey castle across the river from the palace, he was planning another perfidious plot against the King.

'Curse his miserable Majesty a million times, only it would take too long,' he growled. 'I will defeat him somehow. But how? I must plan a plot of such incredible ingenuity that it cannot fail, a crime of which they can't convict me, a felony that can't be found out.'

But that wanted a bit of doing.

'No use sending him a box of chocolates with a bomb in it. The bomb might not go off, or it might go bang at the wrong time or the wrong person. No good writing rude words on his front gate. It isn't drastic enough, and I might get caught as I was when I rang the palace front door bell on Christmas Eve and ran away before they could open it.' That had annoyed the Count, because he had been made to sing *Good King Wenceslas* eight times for pretending to be a carol singer.

He plotted and planned. He looked up books on villains and their nefarious nastiness. He listened to frightful plays on the radio, but they didn't give him any ideas, only a few headaches. But at last one breakfast-time he had an idea. It was so horrible it made the milk in his coffee go sour and unpuffed his puffed cereal.

'My word!' he cried. 'This can't possibly fail. And they can never find out who dun it, I mean, did it.' And, without stopping to finish his egg or have any marmalade, he waited until it was dark. Then he rowed across the river to where the twenty-one guns were standing, loaded with gunpowder and roses, in special cartridges so that the roses shouldn't be burnt when the gunpowder went off.

It was the night before the King's birthday and there was nobody about. All the people were having parties and wishing the King more happy returns than he could possibly need. The soldiers were either practising their birthday parade or polishing themselves up to look extra special. Even the sentries who were usually on guard outside the palace were attending a meeting to learn a special birthday way of presenting arms so that they could be sure of doing it without falling over.

But, beside the guns, there was one sentry standing in a sentry box. He was there to cover up the guns if it rained. He was also there in case anyone got so enthusiastic at a party that he came and tried to let off the guns. But as it was a fine night, and everybody was having too much fun at the parties to think about guns, the sentry found it a bit boring.

'If I didn't have to be here,' he was saying to himself, 'I could be having fun at a party. That is to say, if I didn't have to be learning the special birthday way of presenting arms. Oh dear, a soldier's life is a bit hard.'

Just then there was a loud *bong*, and everything went even blacker than the usual night-time black.

The crafty Count had crept up behind the sentry box and pushed it over, so that it came down like an enormous lid over the sentry and fastened him down like a sausage under a dish cover.

'Help!' he cried. 'Turn out the guard!' He struggled but the sentry box was too heavy to move and there was no one to hear his cries.

'Now,' chuckled the Baron, 'to carry out my plan.' He ran to the ammunition store and began to carry out his plan, which was a bit tiring because it meant carrying out cannon balls. He staggered across with one to the first gun and rolled it into the barrel.

'One,' he panted, making a mark on the ground.

Then back he went, and came out with a second cannon ball.

'Two,' he grunted, after putting the cannon ball into the second gun; and he made another mark on the ground. Then he went on staggering out with one cannon ball after another, dropping them into the twenty-one guns prepared for the King's birthday salute, and marking each one on the ground to that he wouldn't miss any of the guns.

At last every gun was loaded with a deadly, heavy cannon ball on top of the roses. How dastardly! When the guns were fired for the royal salute those cannon balls would go, *boom*, into the palace and the King and Queen who would be standing on the balcony.

'Ah, ha!' chuckled the Count, and he went craftily

THE BIRTHDAY PLOT 71

back to his grim, grey castle for a grim, grey gloat over what he had done.

'They can't catch me this time,' he grunted. 'Nobody will know who did it. I'm safe and the King is doomed. Ha, ha, ha!' And he sat up all the rest of the night drinking dastardly drinks, and gloating ghastly gloats, which is bad for you, but he didn't care.

However, his plan wasn't entirely secret. What the crafty Count didn't know was that there was a little hole in the side of the sentry box, where a knot in the wood had come out. And through this hole the sentry, trapped under the box, had watched the Count carrying out his dastardly plan with the cannon balls. But there wasn't anything the sentry could do. He couldn't get out because the sentry box was too heavy. And presently he got so tired with struggling that he fell fast asleep.

Next day the birthday celebrations were raging with enormous success. Everybody had eaten too much, flags were being waved with enthusiasm as well as with hands. Hats were being thrown up in the air and coming down on the wrong heads, but nobody minded, not even those who got back a cheaper hat than they'd thrown up. What did hats matter when it was the King's birthday?

'What a lovely day!' said the King, as he rode luxuriously along in the royal coach, waving to the populace.

'Why don't we come back by river?' said the Queen. 'It would be rather fun to be rowed along in the royal barge.'

So orders were sent to the Keeper of the Royal Barge to get it out, and launch it, and dust it, and polish it up, and get all the royal watermen dressed in their royal clothes.

'Ah,' said the Lord Chamberlain. 'This gives me an idea. Instead of waiting for Their Majesties to come out on the balcony of the palace, we'll have the royal salute fired across the river as they return. Then the roses will drop all around them like a floral shower. Most agreeable.'

And so he sent instructions to the Captain of the Guard, who ordered out the guards right in the middle of their lunch break to turn the twenty-one guns round so that they faced across the river. The guards were in such a hurry that none of them noticed the sentry box lying on its side. And the sentry was still fast asleep underneath.

Things were terrible! When the guns fired the royal salute, twenty-one heavy, red-hot, cannon balls would go hurtling at the royal barge. It would be sunk.

No wonder the cruel Count Bakwerdz was gloating in his grim castle. He didn't know the guns had been turned round, but he wouldn't have cared. This was going to be even worse than his own plot. He would have been delighted.

'A very successful birthday, my dear,' said the King to the Queen, as they stepped into the royal barge. Then they changed places several times because the Queen could never make up her mind whether to sit on the port side, so that she could enjoy the beautiful scenery, or on the starboard side, where she had a better view of the ducks.

Then the royal watermen bent to their oars and the royal barge went gliding along the river with the royal swans swimming gracefully on either side.

Up in his grim, grey castle above the river the Count was still gloating. Down below on the river bank the Captain of the Guard was drawing his sword as the royal barge approached.

'Prepare to fire the royal salute!' he cried, waving his sword and nearly knocking his hat off. 'One to be ready,

THE BIRTHDAY PLOT

two to be steady ...' The gunners got ready to fire, and everybody else put their fingers in their ears ready for the twenty-one bangs.

'Three to be off!' cried the Captain of the Guard. 'Fire!'

And *boom! crash! bong!* went twenty-one guns, rapidly one after the other. And the twenty-one cannon balls went hurtling towards the royal barge.

'Ow!' cried the Captain of the Guard. 'Stop!' And the gunners went running backwards and forwards, not knowing what to do, while three of the royal watermen fell overboard for safety.

But good gracious! There was something the Count hadn't thought of! The roses that were in the guns dropped prettily all round the royal barge. But the terrible, red-hot cannon balls were much heavier than the roses, and so of course they didn't fall in the same place.* They went whizzing on and on, right across the river and straight into the grim, grey walls of the Count's grim, grey castle, smashing them to grim, grey powder, just as the Count was in the middle of an extra horrid gloat.

'Hurray!' roared the crowd, twice over. Once to cheer the King on his birthday as the roses fell round the royal barge, and once because the cannon balls had passed harmlessly over his head and he was safe. 'Hurray!' they cried. 'Many happy returns to His Majesty!'

'Well,' said the King, 'if that's what you call a happy return I shall come back the other way next time!'

'Majesty! Majesty!' cried the Lord Chamberlain, running up. 'I have discovered it was Count Bakwerdz who put the cannon balls into the guns!' The noise of the guns had woken the sentry, and he had banged on the sides of

* Try for yourself throwing a ball and a piece of paper together, and you'll see what happened.

the sentry box so much that the guards had heard him. He had been rescued and had revealed the Count's dastardly plot.

'The Count must be executed!' said the Lord Chamberlain. 'He has plotted against the Crown before, but this time he has plotted against Your Majesty's life.'

'Oh well,' said the King, who was too kind-hearted to have anyone executed, 'his plot has come down on his own head well and truly this time. Let him live in the ruins of his castle. That will be punishment enough, especially when it rains. But make sure he never comes anywhere near the palace,' he added.

'Or the guns,' put in the Queen. 'In fact, I think this royal salute business is getting a bit risky. In future we'll have the royal salute on twenty-one church bells. It will be nearly as noisy, but more musical and considerably safer.'

10

The Merry Ministers

THE ministers of Incrediblania were, on the whole, a jolly lot. The Lord Chief Justice could imitate various musical instruments. The Prime Minister played the mouth organ. The Lord Chancellor could whistle through his teeth. And all the others were given to getting up to larks of various kinds.

'Look here, this has absolutely got to stop!' said the King, when he came into the council chamber one day and found the ministers throwing paper balls at one another. 'We can't have this, we really can't.'

'Oh, don't be such a spoil-sport!' said the Minister of Education. 'Why shouldn't we have a game or two when there isn't much ruling to do?'

'Well,' said the King, who didn't mind a game or two himself, 'that's all very well, but you know the Queen won't have it.'

'Oo-er, no,' said the Minister of Education, who was very scared of the Queen. 'Suppose she comes in and catches us throwing paper balls about . . .' He started to shake in his shoes and all the other ministers shook in theirs, except for the Prime Minister, who had taken his shoes off to play hopscotch.

'Well, there you are,' said the King. 'You had better stop this playing about, because if the Queen does catch you you'll be for it, and no mistake!'

'I only hope they do stop,' said the King to himself in his private royal thinking room. 'If the Queen catches them, I shall be for it as well as them. She'll say, aren't I the

THE MERRY MINISTERS

King and why don't I stop this nonsense? She'll want to know if I'm a King or a mouse, and I'd really be better off if I were a mouse, because the Queen is scared of mice and wouldn't dare to tell one off for playing about. Of course, I could get the Court Magician to change me into a mouse, and then the Queen would faint at the sight of me. But that wouldn't help much, because I don't like eating the sort of things mice eat and I might get caught in a mouse trap. And having the Queen faint every time she saw me would get tiring. No, no, I must think of some way of stopping the ministers from playing about.'

He sank back in his chair exhausted after all that furious thinking. Then he rang for a cup of coffee and a cream bun, and felt well enough to start thinking again.

'It's very awkward,' he thought. 'I can't think of a way of stopping the ministers playing about and I can't ask advice about it because the only people who can advise me are the ministers. Oh dear, being a king isn't all coffee and cream buns.' But he ordered another one of each anyway.

Meanwhile, in the council chamber the ministers had stopped playing about. But only to think of some way of making sure the Queen didn't catch them playing about.

'We could tie a bell on the Queen's shoe. Then we'd hear her coming and be able to stop playing about before she caught us,' said the Lord Chancellor.

'Good idea, said the Prime Minister. 'Who's going to volunteer to tie the bell on the Queen's shoe? How about you?' he said to the Lord Chancellor. 'It was your idea, you know.'

'I, er, er, I can't tie very good knots,' said the Lord Chancellor.

And the other ministers couldn't tie very good knots either, or didn't understand bells, or felt it wasn't a good idea, because tying a bell on the Queen's shoe would have been rather like tying a ribbon round a tiger's neck.

'Perhaps we could appoint someone to keep watch,' said the Lord Chief Justice, 'and warn us when the Queen was coming.'

But nobody was willing to keep watch in case the Queen caught them keeping watch and wanted to know what they were keeping watch for, which was exactly the kind of thing the Queen would have wanted to know.

Then the Prime Minister suddenly had a bright idea.

'Listen!' he said. 'We have agreed that we cannot tie a bell on the Queen's shoe. So let us all tie bells on our own shoes. Then when we hear someone coming, and there's no bell going *ting ting* as they walk, we shall know it isn't one of us, and that it is probably the Queen. And we can stop playing about and pretend to be working.'

'Of course, it might not be the Queen,' said the Lord Chief Justice, who had a very legal mind and liked arguing things out. 'It might only be the maid with our morning coffee.'

'Well, it doesn't matter,' said the Prime Minister. 'We would have to stop playing about to drink our coffee anyway.'

'And we don't want anyone else to know we play about,' said the Lord Chamberlain, 'in case the Queen hears of it.'

So they all tied little bells on their shoes, so that they could hear one another coming and know it wasn't the Queen.

Back in his royal thinking room the King still hadn't thought of a way of stopping the ministers playing about.

So he gave up and came out of the room just as the Prime Minister went by.

'Hullo!' said the King. 'What's all this *ting ting* business? Why have you got little bells on your shoes?'

'Well, er, I, that is to say,' stammered the Prime Minister. None of the ministers had thought what to say if they were asked that question. 'I, er, it is a little idea of mine,' he said, thinking fast, 'for, er, letting Your Majesty know where we are,' he finished.

'Well, you'd better not let the Queen catch you wearing bells on your shoes,' said the King, 'or she'll want to know why, and probably forbid it.'

'Coo, yes!' said the Prime Minister. 'We hadn't thought of that. It won't do to let Her Majesty know about the bells or . . .' He stopped before he said too much, but it was already too late.

'Or what?' asked the King. 'Now, look here,' he said. 'What's the game? Come on, tell me and it had better not be treason.'

'Er, er, well Majesty,' said the Prime Minister, and he told the King about the ministers all tying bells on their shoes, so that, if they heard someone coming without a bell, they could stop playing in case it was the Queen.

'Ha!' said the King. 'Very clever, I'm sure. But serve you right if the Queen gets to know about it, that's all.'

The Prime Minister went hurrying back to the other ministers, and told them what the King had said.

'We hadn't thought of that,' he added. 'If the Queen starts wanting to know about the bells she'll tell us not to have them.'

'We must wear our shoes with the bells only when we're on our way to the council chamber,' said the Lord Chief Justice. 'Then the Queen isn't likely to spot them.'

The King was taking a stroll in the rose garden when suddenly he thought of an idea.

Next day he stopped the Lord Chancellor on his way to the council chamber.

'Ah, my dear Lord Chancellor,' he said, 'pray come and have breakfast with me. There is something I want you to do.'

The Lord Chancellor had already had an enormous

breakfast, but he couldn't refuse the King's invitation. He rattled his knife and fork about among the kippers, pretending to eat. The King didn't notice, he was too busy carrying out his idea.

'What I want you to do,' he said, 'is take a little trip to the next kingdom ... er, pardon me!' As he said this he knocked his knife off the table.

'I'll get it for you, Majesty,' said the Lord Chancellor.

'No no, don't trouble,' said the King. He got down under the table, picked up the knife, and secretly cut the bell off one of the Lord Chancellor's shoes.

'... to the next kingdom,' he repeated, getting out from under the table. And went on to explain what he wanted the Lord Chancellor to do there, but all he really wanted was to get the Lord Chancellor out of the way for a time.

As soon as the Lord Chancellor had left the palace the King went along and dropped the bell in the passage just outside the Queen's boudoir. Then he went away to await events.

'Bless me! What is this, may I ask?' said the Queen, coming out of her boudoir and seeing the bell lying on the floor. 'We can't have bells left lying about all over the palace. I shall have to do something about it.'

She set off for the royal council chamber to tell off the Lord Chamberlain, so that he would tell off the Housekeeper, to make her tell off the Head Housemaid, so that she would tell off the under maids for not sweeping up properly.

And as she walked along she kept going *ting ting* with the bell, wondering where on earth it had come from. And the ministers in the council chamber, hearing her coming, thought it was one of them.

'It's the Lord Chancellor,' said the Prime Minister. 'All the rest of us are here, so it must be him.'

So all the ministers screwed up bits of paper and got ready to pelt the Lord Chancellor as soon as he opened the door.

'Ready?' cried the Prime Minister, as the door opened. 'Let her go!'

And *swish!* a shower of screwed-up paper balls hit the Queen as she came in. They knocked her crown crooked, they got in her hair. But the ministers got in her hair even worse.

'Help!' cried the ministers. And they all didn't know what to do with themselves, except for the Lord Chamberlain, who dived into the waste paper basket and got stuck there.

For a moment there was a blood-curdling silence, for the Queen was so majestically furious she couldn't think of what to say, which was so unusual that it made her even fiercer. Then she did think of what to say, and she said it. She told the ministers what she thought of them. She told them their fortunes in a way that made the future look as black as a dark coal cellar. She talked those poor ministers off their heads, and round and round and back again. She went on at them. She made them wish they had never been ministers, and some of them wished they didn't exist.

'For this shocking behaviour,' she said finally, 'you will all write out the laws of Incrediblania . . . and make them rhyme too. And any more of this nonsense and off with your heads!' And off she stalked, leaving the ministers collapsed all over the floor.

Outside in the corridor the Queen came on the King laughing fit to split his robes.

'And what, may I ask, is so funny?' she said.

'Oh, nothing, my dear,' chuckled the King. 'I've just remembered a very funny joke you told me last month.'

'Oh I see,' said the Queen, feeling rather flattered that the King had remembered one of her jokes and thought it so funny. And she went off to have a nice cup of tea to recover from being fierce with the ministers.

And the King went on laughing, because he had at last found a way to stop the ministers playing about.

11

Someone at the Door

THERE was a real din going on in the royal palace, because the King's Page was holding on to the handle on one side of a door, and the Queen's Page was holding the handle on the other side. And they were both pulling and tugging, trying to make the other let go.

'Let go! Get away! Yah!' called the Pages to each other rather rudely, as pages do.

Just then along came the King on the side of the door where his Page was.

'Now now, what's going on here?' said His Majesty.

'P-p-p-please, Majesty,' said the Page nervously. 'It's the Queen's Page, Majesty. I'm trying to shut the door, and he's hanging on to the handle on the other side and won't let me.'

'Disgraceful!' cried the King. 'Go round and tell the other Page to let go!'

'Y-y-yes, Majesty,' said the King's Page. And he went, while the King took hold of the door handle and cried, 'Let go at once, do you hear?'

But, strange to say, just at the same moment the Queen had come in on the other side of the door where *her* Page was. And she was most annoyed at the noise he was making.

'Is this the way to behave?' she cried. 'Less of it, at once! None at all of it, in fact. Who is that on the other side of the door, pulling and tugging and helping you to make this noise?'

'I, I, I, that is to say, Majesty,' gabbled the Queen's

Page, shaking like a jelly. 'It's His Majesty's Page, Majesty. I'm trying to open the door, and he keeps trying to keep it shut.'

'Well, go round and tell him to stop it this moment!' cried the Queen. And, as the Page scampered off, all shaky at the knees, Her Majesty took hold of the handle and shook it, calling out, 'Will you let go of this handle this minute?'

But, of course, the King, who was on the other side, didn't know it was the Queen talking to him. So he grew more and more cross, thinking it was the other Page talking.

'Cease this impudence at once!' he cried. 'How dare you! Let go! Do you hear?' And he shook the door more violently than the Pages had done, because he was bigger.

'What's this? What's this?' shrieked the Queen, nearly fainting with rage at hearing what she thought was a Page talk to her like that. 'Open this door at once!' She shook the door too. The din was awful. Much worse than it had been when the Pages were making it.

The two Pages, who had each gone round to the other side of the door to fetch the other, missed each other, because they went different ways. The Queen's Page saw it was the King on the other side, and said, 'Oo-er!' and ran away to hide. And the King's Page, when he found it was Her Majesty on the other side of the door and in a towering rage too, was so frightened that he ran out of the palace without looking where he was going, and fell into a pond of goldfish.

So there were Their two most important Majesties pulling and tugging away at the door, and shouting the most unroyal things at each other, because their voices sounded so strange through the door that they didn't recognize each other.

'Ho, there!' roared the King, beginning to grow tired. 'Fetch the Prime Minister!' And when the Prime Minister came he hung on to the King's arms and helped him pull.

But that didn't help because the Queen had called for the Lord Chamberlain, and he was helping *her* pull. All that happened was that the din and noise became worse.

Then the King called for the Lord Chief Justice, and the Queen for the Lord Chancellor.

'Call the guard!' panted the King. But the Queen had called for the guard too, and so they got half each and the noise became frightful.

Then the King called for the army and the Queen called for the navy. Battalions and regiments came and joined in the tug-of-war. Shiploads and crews of sailors pulled on the other side. There were so many of them they stretched right across the room, through the corridors, out of the palace and across the grounds.

Bang, bang, went the door. 'Yo ho, heave, ho!' cried the sailors. And the soldiers, not having any heaving song, all said, 'Gr-r-r!' because it was the fiercest thing they knew.

Then suddenly the King caught sight of the Queen's page, who had just finished pulling the other Page out of the goldfish pond.

'Oh,' he said. 'So you've let go at last, have you?' And, letting go of the handle himself, he marched the Page off to show him what was what.

And, of course, the second he let go, the door flew open and the Queen sat down, bump! And she knocked over the Lord Chamberlain, who fell against the Lord Chan-

SOMEONE AT THE DOOR 89

cellor, who knocked the guards over like ninepins, and they made the navy go down, bump, bump, all along the line, out of the palace and through the grounds.

'What's the meaning of this?' cried the Queen. She got up in a worse temper than ever, and strode through the door. But nobody was there. The Prime Minister and Lord Chief Justice had gone to have tea, and the guards had dismissed, and the army had gone away to drill.

'Bless me!' she exclaimed, rubbing her eyes. 'Can I have imagined someone was pulling the door?' She turned round to ask the Lord Chamberlain, but he and the Lord Chancellor had picked themselves up and gone away, and her half of the guards had dismissed, and the sailors had gone back to their ships, all thinking the trouble was over and they weren't wanted any more. So there was the Queen all by herself.

'Dear, dear me,' she said. 'I can't have myself seeing things that don't exist. I must have been ruling too hard or something. I shall go for a nice little holiday by the sea.'

And the King didn't say anything about the door-pulling because it would have made him look rather silly; the army and navy and guards were too busy to say anything, and, of course, the Pages didn't dare breathe a word.

But nobody ever pulls at doors in the palace now; they tap ever so carefully and open the door a tiny bit to see if everything's all right on the other side. Some of the very nervous ones won't open a door at all; if it's shut they go round and climb through the windows.

12

Incrediblania Nearly Undone

'A PARCEL for Your Majesty,' announced the Butler, bowing low while a footman brought in an exciting-looking package.

'A letter for Your Majesty,' cried the Chief Herald, saluting heraldically while the Assistant Herald brought in an ornamental envelope on a tray.

'A gentleman to see Your Majesty,' said the Lord Chamberlain, and in strode a brisk person in red top boots.

'Trouble always comes in threes,' said the King. 'We can't do everything at once, you know, even though we are a king. Give the gentleman in the red boots a cup of cocoa and one of the Queen's rock cakes. That will keep him busy while I open my parcel and read my letter.'

He cut the string and tore open the parcel. It contained a big black bag and a small white note.

Dear Majesty, (said the note)
Be good enough to fill this bag with gold and leave it by the third oak tree outside the palace gates tonight at midnight. If you don't, I shall destroy your kingdom, burn down your palace, and eat all your subjects.
Yours obediently, Brimstone Junior, Superior Dragon.

'But this is ridiculous,' cried the King. 'We got rid of all the dragons in Incrediblania long ago!'

'Yes, I remember,' said the Queen. 'And you gave orders that no dragons were to be slain, and the dragons found it wasn't much fun not being hunted so they went away.'

'Ah,' said the Prime Minister. 'That was all very well in those days but dragons have been getting a bit out of hand lately, I've heard. You can't go on being lenient with dragons, you know. I think we shall have to do away with that law saying dragons mustn't be slain.'

But the King wasn't listening. He had just finished reading the letter the Chief Herald had brought in, and he was waving his hands and moaning, 'Oh, oh, oh, disaster!' and 'Oh, I wish I wasn't King!'

For the letter was from His Extreme Altitude, the Nabob of Nullipop, who had written to say he was coming for a short visit to Incrediblania, and was bringing two other Oriental potentates with him, on a tour arranged by *The Association of Oriental Monarchs for Foreign Visits to Enlarge Acquaintance with Unusual Food and Curious Customs.* They would be arriving at any minute.

'This is terrible!' cried the King. '*Three* Oriental potentates! Didn't I just say trouble always comes in threes? If we don't pay off the dragon he'll attack the kingdom, and, when the Oriental monarchs arrive and find everything in a mess, they'll be so annoyed they'll start a war!'

'Yes,' said the Prime Minister, who was very good at guessing the worst, 'and, if we do pay off the dragon, we shan't have enough money left to entertain the Oriental monarchs with the lavishness they'll expect, and they'll make war just the same!'

'Oh dear, don't say we're undone?' cried the Queen.

'Pardon, Majesty,' said the person in red boots, who had finished his cocoa and pushed the Queen's rock cake secretly into a fern pot. 'Pardon, Majesty, but I can solve your problem. I came to offer Your Majesty my services in case of need and it seems there is need. Promise me the hand of the Princess in marriage, and I will slay the dragon.'

'Oh, shut up!' said the King. 'You can't slay the dragon because we have a law against it, and you can't have the hand of the Princess because all our Princesses are already married. And,' he turned to the Queen, 'don't say your Aunt Emily has a spare daughter. I'm tired of giving away princesses, real or adopted, as if they were gift packets at a supermarket.'

'All right, Majesty,' said Red Boots. 'If you will alter the law about slaying dragons, I will slay this one for the usual half kingdom reward.'

'Oh, all right!' said the King, not thinking much of the plan, but having no idea at all of a better one. 'But are you quite sure you can slay the dragon? Suppose he slays you?'

'No fear of that!' cried Red Boots, slapping his chest. 'I shall take him unawares. Listen,' he went on, 'you must put the bag of gold under the third oak tree as the dragon told you, and then, while he's checking it, I shall attack him from the rear.'

But oh, what frightful dishonesty! No wonder Red Boots was so confident. There wasn't any dragon at all. It was all a plot of his to get the bag of gold. He was going to make off with the gold and never be seen again. And three Oriental monarchs due at any moment! Incrediblania was on the edge of being undone.

That night, at midnight, Red Boots went striding bravely to the third oak tree outside the palace gates to slay the dragon he knew wouldn't be there, and to get to gold he expected would be.

'Ha, there it is!' he cried, as he spied the black bag lying by the tree. 'Hum, gold is certainly heavy. Wish I'd brought a bicycle or a wheelbarrow. This is going to take some getting away with.'

INCREDIBLANIA NEARLY UNDONE 93

But suddenly, from behind that very oak tree, came, not a dragon, of course. Oh no, *three* dragons! Didn't the King say trouble always comes in threes? They were real, snorting, smoking dragons. And they made for Red Boots with all their teeth showing.

'Wow!' he shrieked. 'Go away! You aren't here! You can't be! You don't exist! I invented you!'

But whether the dragons existed or not, they set about Red Boots. He shot up the tree, dragging the heavy bag with him. One of the dragons grabbed him but he dropped the bag on its nose. The dragon saw stars and fell back.

Then out of the palace gates came the King. He wanted to make sure Red Boots slew the dragon. When he saw three dragons he couldn't believe his eyes. But the dragons saw the King and turned on him.

Red Boots immediately started climbing down the tree to get the bag of gold. The dragons were nearly on the King.

Then the ground began to shake. But it was not because of the dragons. No, it was the three Oriental potentates, with three elephants each! They dashed to the rescue, and, *crash, thump, boom, wallop,* they set about the dragons.

The elephants were tough as well as heavy, and soon they had stamped all over the dragons. The King and kingdom of Incrediblania were saved once more.

'Hurray! And thanks ever so!' cried the King.

Silken ladders were got out, and red carpets laid down, and the elephants persuaded to sit down nice and quietly so that the potentates could climb down, and the King could shake hands with each of them.

'Now,' said the King, 'where's that Red Boots fellow?'

But Red Boots had come down from the tree as soon as

INCREDIBLANIA NEARLY UNDONE

he saw the dragons were finished, and had made off with the black bag.

'Scoundrel!' roared the King. 'Pilferer! Knave! Varlet! He has stolen the gold! Back to the palace and fetch the army! He must be caught.'

'It is certainly desirable,' said the Nabob of Nullipop. And the other two potentates folded their hands over their tummies, where there was plenty of room for them, and smiled blandly, as Eastern potentates like to do when frantic things are happening to other people.

When they all arrived at the palace, there was the Queen standing on the steps to receive them.

'Welcome to the party!' she cried.

'No, no, no!' whispered the King, frenziedly. 'Cancel party! No money for it! Red Boots was scoundrel. Escaped with bag of gold!'

'No, no!' whispered back the Queen, smiling to the potentates, and bowing, to look polite in spite of the whisperings. 'No gold in bag. I put coal there instead!'

The King was just going to be cheered up at this news when he suddenly thought of something else.

'The potentates!' he gasped. 'Three of them. They have slain the three dragons. That means we must give them half the kingdom each. But three halves into one won't go. It can't be done, so we *are* undone!'

Just then the Herald came rushing up to herald the arrival of three kings from the neighbouring kingdoms. The King of Incrediblania hardly had time to say anything about trouble always coming in threes when the three kings themselves appeared.

'Oh, most noble rescuer!' they chanted. 'Oh, how can we thank you?'

'Er, pardon?' said the King.

'You have rid our three kingdoms of the three terrible

dragons that have been ravaging them. One half of each of our kingdoms is yours as reward.'

What a remarkable thing! The three dragons the potentates had slain had come from the three neighbouring kingdoms!

'This is magnificent!' cried the King. 'It was not I who slew your dragons,' he said to the three kings. 'It was these Eastern gentlemen and their elephants. So your three half kingdoms should go to them. One half each,' he added, to show he was good at arithmetic.

The monarchs were quite willing, but the Eastern potentates said, 'No, no, not at all!' in their own languages, which sounded rather like 'Have a mince pie!' They had so enjoyed the dragon fight, and all the excitement, they thought it was a marvellous welcome to Incrediblania, and they didn't want any reward. Anyway, they said, half a kingdom so far away from their own lands would be very awkward to rule. You can't govern a kingdom by post, not with the cost of postage what it is.

So everything was three times wonderful. The neighbouring kings had got rid of their dragons and didn't have to get rid of half their kingdoms. The Eastern potentates were pleased to be delighted three times over.

And, best of all, the kingdom of Incrediblania was not undone after all.